OSCAR NIEMEYER

THE MASTERS OF
WORLD ARCHITECTURE SERIES

UNDER THE GENERAL EDITORSHIP OF WILLIAM ALEX

oscar niemeyer

by Stamo Papadaki

George Braziller, Inc.
NEW YORK, 1960

CONTENTS

I have long been aware that modern architecture in Brazil is more than a mere aesthetic trend, and above all more than the projection into our culture of a universal movement. It has in fact put at our service the means with which to find the best possible solution of our city planning and housing problems, a solution which carefully takes into account climate and scenery. It is, furthermore, a strong affirmative expression of our culture, perhaps the most original and precise expression of the creative intelligence of modern Brazil.

—JUSCELINO KUBITSCHEK

1. BRAZIL AND THE MODERN ARCHITECTURAL MOVEMENT

ALBERT CAMUS IN THE preface to one of his collections of essays[1] said: "One finds in this world a great deal of injustice but there is one about which no one ever speaks—the injustice of the climate." Having never abandoned the spiritual climate of the Mediterranean shores where he was born and grew up under the dual play of the sun and the sea, Camus felt a deep compassion for those living in the gray, uniform and immovable settings of the industrial centers of the north, the "exile" into which man has been thrown knowing neither the reason, nor the duration, nor the hope for an eventual return to the "kingdom." Moreover, this injustice must affect not only the man who inhabits a hard climate but, also, the architecture which has been erected in his defense. A building can hardly be expected to become a source of emotional impact, a joyous event, when it expresses only an environmental struggle, a minimum condition for survival. The promise of a clear victory of architecture over an aggressive nature becomes very dim as the image of the Hyperborean Apollo disappears into the northern mists.

Architecture is the fruit that matures with the sun; being all of the earth, its life is in the skies, in the light that is the sky and insofar as it becomes light. There is no miraculous metamorphosis of things and functions without a happy climate and no life of architectural forms without geographic prototypes. The earth and the sky are the true materials out of which architecture is made and, hence, it may resemble "the mathematical image of a girl of Corinth" with whom the architect was happily in love.[2] The influence of a given physical milieu upon the arts and in the shaping of the thinking patterns of its inhabitants permeated the philosophy of art of the nineteenth century; it is epitomized in Elie Faure's *The Spirit of Forms,* where mention is made of a "sculptural environment of geographic nature in Greece" and of a "pictorial environment by virtue of the atmosphere in Holland." Brazil offers a rich geomorphic background and climatic conditions that are far from aggressive. The rate of change in both geographic forms and qualities of climate is, however, slower than is to be found in the Mediterranean basin. Lenormant, describing an area approximately eighteen by twenty-five miles situated on the Gulf of Tarentum, in southern Italy, said: "Everything is united there, the joyous greenery of the environs of Naples, the grandeur of the most majestic Alpine landscapes, the sun and the sea of Greece," and added that the flora includes not only the evergreens of northern Europe but also the laurel, the olive and the fig tree.[3] Such a microcosm is alien in Brazil where land masses are on the scale of a continent and the climate gradually changes from tropical to temperate with occasional snowfalls. Between the north and the south of Brazil there are more than thirty-eight degrees of latitude. Its land area is larger than that of the continental United States but its coast line is shorter by about two hundred miles. High temperatures vary from 100.4° F. in Sena Madureira to 77.36° F. in Pôrto Alegre, which averages a low temperature of 59.16° F. Over 60 per cent of the territory is a series of stepped plateaus surrounded by alluvial valleys. This abstract description of a country rendered in measured quantities should be of no direct value for the one who wants to know the shape and the color ranges of the land, the quality of the air as it is breathed or felt on the skin, the smell of the rocks and the vegetation, the particular ways of the growing things. But certain aspects of those "quantities" which comprise the reality of Brazil were to have an important influence on the development of its modern movement in architecture. Without this particular knowledge—the narrow temperature range and the nature and extent of the land masses of Brazil—it would be difficult to comprehend the "native" building scale that is in use there. This scale is equally different from the gigantism (vertical or horizontal) which is to be found in the United States and from the parochial miniaturism which prevails in southern Europe; it has confounded and often irritated a number of architectural visitors from the mother Latin Countries.

In addition to the physical aspects of the country we must consider the particular local character of certain attitudes of the people. Max Weber, on the basis of a text by Benjamin Franklin, presented the concept or belief that work alone is the only possible redemption for man on this earth in the face of the apparent indifference of a distant God; and that the resulting economic advantages were not incompatible with the Protestant ethic.[4] The active "pursuit of happiness," a prime mover of the people of the United States, could be well contrasted with the taste for the "good life" which permeates Brazil. This good life is of the present and is continuously present, not to be achieved only after a desperate struggle, since nature is not an enemy and man's earthly condition does not depend wholly on his inevitable death. From its early days, Brazil was identified with one of the never-never lands which, since the Middle Ages, were invented before they had been discovered.[5] The land of the "good Indians," the "Naturvölkern" who live in harmony with nature and outside of the "original sin," attracted the attention of those who sought the vestiges of an earthly paradise and was often used as a backdrop to Utopias. This conditioned European literature in the eighteenth century and overflowed into the first part of the nineteenth. In our century we have the notebooks of Paul Gauguin.

The social aspects of Brazil as a very active and efficient melting pot attracted the attention of a number of sociologists.[6] There is a wealth of excellent material on the subject; Jean Lambert mentions the coexistence of two Brazils, the modern and the archaic but this should not be understood in the narrow sense of an advanced or a retarded mechanization, or as an uneven penetration of the industrial movement. A far richer image could be achieved if it were seen with C. G. Jung as the superimposition of the historical man upon the archaic.

The sculptural, variegated landscapes of Brazil, a climate which demands a minimum of technological assistance, a way of life which depends on a presence rather than on an ambiguous flux of becoming and a people with a rich emotional capacity which in its outward form becomes lyric poetry while its inner form bends towards archetypes—these may explain some facets of the flowering of the new Brazilian architecture.

The rapid and vigorous growth of the modern architectural movement in Brazil cannot be fully explained by a strict economic determinism or historical materialism. In the absence of a building industry, without any ground preparation by local architectural pioneers and with a school guided by nineteenth-century academicism, the period of initiation and the public acceptance of the modern movement practically overlapped. A Russian, born Gregory Warchavchik, in São Paulo, and a

"Carioca"[7] architect, Lucio Costa, could be placed at the beginnings of the movement, if beginnings and growth can be differentiated in such a short span of time. The former in 1925 published in a local newspaper his *Manifesto of Functional Architecture*—reprinted a few months later in the Rio de Janeiro press; in this he preceded by seven years Alberto Sartoris who, with his book *The Elements of Functional Architecture,* is generally considered the father of the term "functional."[8] Lucio Costa was at that time appointed director of the National School of Fine Arts which then included the School of Architecture. In spite of the short duration of his directorship, Costa introduced a number of reforms which had lasting effects upon the formation of the younger Brazilian architects. There is also the direct (his short visits to Brazil) and indirect (his books) influence of Le Corbusier. In 1925 the last issues of the *Esprit Nouveau* were published and four volumes of its *Collection* were on sale in the newly erected pavilion bearing the name of the magazine at the International Exposition of Decorative Arts in Paris. In 1927 the explosive incident of the competition for the League of Nations Headquarters took place, attracting world-wide attention to Le Corbusier's project which was placed *hors concours* on the basis that it had not been drawn with India ink. By this time the name of Le Corbusier was thoroughly familiar in the Latin American countries, in the USSR and in Central Europe. In order to comprehend the overwhelming appeal exerted by his writings we should see them as being quite apart from his creative work as an architect. Le Corbusier as an author and pamphleteer addressed himself to those countries approaching or about to cross the threshold of industrialization. Insisting, and rightly, that architecture should be at the basis of the "mechanical equipment" of a country—a term recurrent in his writings —he presented architecture as an alternate to revolution.[9] Elie Faure, as a student of the past, had said that when societies were retooling themselves architecture took the lead. Closer to Auguste Comte and the nineteenth-century positivist movement than to Descartes—there is hardly an element of doubt in Le Corbusier but there is, perhaps, the equivalent: a fresh, unprejudiced approach to a problem—he was able to present clear and reasonable programs for action. It is interesting to note that Brazilian disciples of Comte and his early geopolitics were, during the last century, the most ardent proponents of the idea of moving the capital of Brazil from the coast to the hinterland of Goiás—approximately where the new capital, Brasilia, is now located. As long as the plastic work of Le Corbusier remains highly personal, often inaccessible, at times hermetic, closer to Picasso's dialectics of seeking or finding, and, also the most youthful and fresh among a quivering architectural avant-garde, it is in his writings alone that we should look for the roots of his enormous influence. And it is in his dual ability as a poet and a slogan maker that we should find the reasons for the uneven results of that influence.

Le Corbusier first visited Brazil in 1929, lecturing in São Paulo and Rio de Janeiro during a tour which included Argentina and Uruguay[10]; his second visit took place in 1936 at the invitation of the Brazilian Minister of Education, Gustavo Capanema. Working for about a month with Lucio Costa and a small group of younger Brazilian architects which included Oscar Niemeyer, he developed two schemes for the Ministry of Education Building, corresponding to two different sites, and also the layout for a new campus for the National University of Brazil. It was then that he reminded his collaborators of the existence and the potential of the "azulejo"—the Portuguese blue ceramic tile which was identified only with old colonial buildings and purely sentimental values—as a worthy finishing material.[11] From that time the modern architectural movement in Brazil started to gather momentum. Beginning with occasional scattered avant-garde demonstrations, it gradually acquired coherence and self-reliance and, finally, was able to dominate the scene. The two decades that followed were imbued with the most ardent architectural optimism, a kind of creative lust which permeated architects, clients, public administrators, the man in the street and the visiting Indian. In an era generally marked by fratricide—partial or total—in the gloom of the historical man who faces not the end of history but of himself, it is hard for one to believe that architecture could again be a source of exuberance. So powerful was the "vital impulse" of an initially small group of men![12]

"When the peaks of our sky join together again—my house will have a roof."

—PAUL ELUARD

2. THE BEGINNINGS

WE DO NOT KNOW if the young man who at the age of twenty-three entered the National School of Fine Arts in Rio de Janeiro to study architecture had at that time the "vague and confused presentiment of his destiny" which Lucio Costa was to feel two years later when Niemeyer started to work in his office. But, the latter's insistence on being entrusted with difficult professional tasks at an early stage can be understood only in the light of later developments, and may now be interpreted as a creative eagerness ready to explode rather than as a youthful impatience.

Oscar Niemeyer Soares Filho was born of a well-to-do family on the 15th of December, 1907, in Rio de Janeiro. His older brother became a physician, a brain specialist with an international reputation. Having finished the Barnabitas College and already married, Niemeyer started his architectural studies in 1930. Long before his graduation in 1934, he became the father of a daughter. Ana Maria Niemeyer Attademo, now an interior designer, often collaborates with her father. This was a period of great upheaval in the architectural school, with prolonged students' strikes and forceful attempts to revitalize the curriculum—expressions of the awakening of a national consciousness permeating the architectural ranks. While a student, Niemeyer offered to join the office of Lucio Costa in preference to any other architectural firm and showed a tenacious insistence in defense of his choice, an insistence that at the time was somewhat puzzling to Lucio Costa.[13] It seems that Niemeyer's work in the office had no particular distinction and passed unnoticed until 1936, when Le Corbusier came as an adviser for the design of the Ministry of Education Building. Then, a complete transformation took place in the young architect: was it the result of a newly acquired clarity of scope or the sensing of the reality of a destiny? Speculation on such events is difficult as they usually imply a state of grace, the effects of a miraculous revelation, or the pre-existence of latent forces which are activated into a sudden maturity of purpose, into a fulgent moment of consciousness. It should not be incorrect, however, to say that this impact was not so much of artistic mastery but, rather, of intellectual integrity, of an ethical awareness which gives someone the strength and ability to say "no." Le Corbusier often used to say that talent was not enough if it could not be backed by a strong character; and many young men departed from his studio with only a set of "stilts" and "roof gardens" while others, in a state of perpetual rage, were to develop complicated roof systems and flat, ground-bound buildings.

In that same year of Le Corbusier's visit, Niemeyer began to work independently on a number of architectural projects. In 1939, after the withdrawal of Lucio Costa, he was elected head of the design group for the Ministry of Education Building; and since then he has maintained his own practice except for the period between the years 1957–1960 when he served as chief architect for the Building Authority of Brasilia, Novacap. Niemeyer's professional career presents a unique characteristic: a continuous, undisturbed and serene development of his creative abilities. While many of the pioneers of the previous generation suffered long and often critical interruptions of their building activity, owing to world-wide or topical vicissitudes and to strong reactionary pressures of the respective "authorities," it seems that Niemeyer enjoyed the full trust of the temporal powers. The heads of municipalities from Recife in the north of Pôrto Alegre in the southernmost tip of Brazil were commissioning him to draw large recreational schemes and building complexes to adorn their cities and enhance the local civic spirit. Thus, Niemeyer designed a tremendous number of buildings (projects and actual buildings[14]) and at one particular period he had over sixty commissions on the drafting boards. To present his complete works would require several volumes; we attempt here to present a few —it is difficult even to say the most characteristic. The choice here is based on those buildings which appeal to the unpredictable public, on those with an unusual content or program and, finally, on those solutions which by their particular character are identified as Niemeyer's personal contribution to modern architecture.

One of Niemeyer's earliest projects, drawn in 1936, is for the house of Henrique Xavier in Rio de Janeiro. Bound by two party walls on the sides and with only a "front" and "back," this house is developed on four levels. The plans present very little kinship with each other (figure 1). What appears remarkable in this solution is the independent growth of the spatial elements of each level in different directions and the placement of volumes over voids (figures 2, 3); also, the solution provides without any loss in continuity, open-air living space on all levels in a variety of shapes and orientations. Here we have an intuitive and, perhaps, rough image of the dwelling-tree which was expressed earlier but with a strong classical restraint in the Savoy house by Le Corbusier and which, twenty years later, was to find a full realization on six distinct levels in the "Villa Shodan" in Ahmedabad, India, by the same architect (figure 4). In this project of Niemeyer's the plastic idiom follows the general trends of the time with emphasis on directness of means rather than on invention or novelty. It is behind this unassuming façade that we find

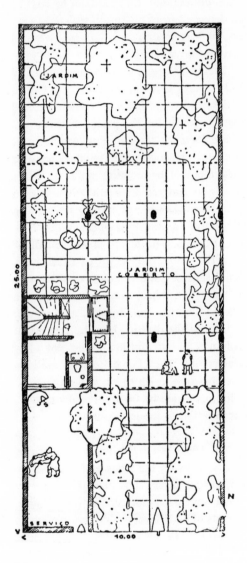

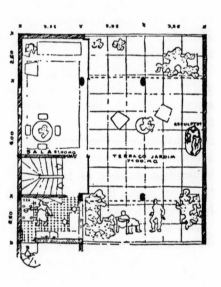

one of the great cosmic images, the tree, with all its oneiric potential of ascension, flight, return and regeneration.[15] Height as an aerial quality, as a condition of the imagination in action within the realm of the four substances—fire, air, water and earth, to follow the sequence of the alchemists—and not as a simple space co-ordinate becomes with Niemeyer a very important plastic theme. "Verticalizing" images, that is to say images suggesting movements of flight towards aerial summits and towards the light, of Icarian content, are to be found with remarkable persistence in lyric poetry (Shelley, Rilke); during the last forty years they became means

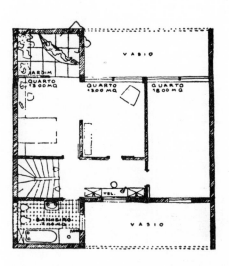 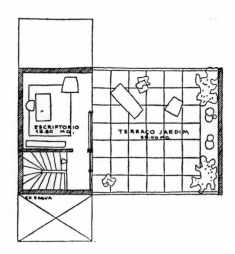

Figure 1. Henrique Xavier House, Rio de Janeiro, 1936. Ground floor plan (far left), first floor plan (left), second and third floor plans (above)

Figure 2.   Henrique Xavier House. Section

Figure 3.   Henrique Xavier House. Perspective sketch by Niemeyer

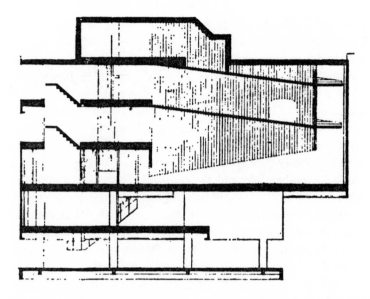

Figure 4.   Le Corbusier, Villa Shodan, Ahmedabad, India, 1956. Section

of therapy with Dr. Robert Desoille's* ascensional treatment of emotional complexes. This imagery, however, is not common in contemporary architecture
and a great number of buildings are meant to be flat, shallow and ground-bound
assemblies. Simplicity of means, a directness of purpose and solutions so natural, so
inevitable as to appear almost automatic to the layman, also permeate Niemeyer's
later work—the result of a distillation of thought or of an action of archetypes.

The first of Niemeyer's buildings actually to be built was a maternity clinic
situated on the shores of the lagoon of Rodrigos de Frietas in Rio de Janeiro
(plates 65, 66). Designed in 1937 for a philanthropic institution ("Obra de
Berco") which provides free medical assistance and guidance for future mothers
and mothers with infants, this building with its bare contours satisfactorily reflects
the modest financial means of the institution and the desire to obtain a friendly,
anti-institutional atmosphere. In spite of the complicated program calling for
separate circulation for patients, medical staff and welfare personnel, an auditorium
for lectures and film showings and a large nursery room occupying the entire third
floor and extending to a roof garden, the solution presents the aspect of a modest
house. The only animation occurs on the northern façade where a sunbreak[16] of
vertical, adjustable louvers for each of the three upper floors creates a play of light

* The psychosynthetic technique of Dr. Robert Desoille applied in many Swiss clinics is
  described in his book, *Exploration de l'Affectivité Subconsciente par la Méthode du Rêve
  Eveillé*, Artrey, Paris, 1938.

and shadow—the legitimate substance of architecture. By virtue of the adjustable louvers the façade offers an endless incidental variety within an orderly frame. The transformation of a rather complicated, often heterogeneous (one is tempted to say non-homologous) content which contemporary civilization imposes as a building program, into a coherent unit through the ordering action of the architect—the unity in the complex as in *imago mundi*—can be seen here and in the entire work of Niemeyer. This transformation suggests a miraculous return to the atemporal times when the action of building was identified with cosmogonic rites, when a structure was to embody the rhythms and the meaning of Cosmos—all that is in the order of the incomprehensible and the revealed—instead of translating, in spatial terms, temporal programmatic demands and technological prescriptions of the day.

On the opposite shores of the same lagoon rises the "Sul America" built by Niemeyer twenty years later (plates 67–69); a surging structure of ten floors, it provides the facilities of a general hospital. Although there is an enormous difference in size compared with the maternity clinic, and although the hospital is implanted on the grounds with greater ease, the same ordering force is evident. One may look here in vain for the painful assemblage of nursing and therapy units, surgery, out-patient department and morgue which in a modern hospital make up an incongruous mass without a beginning or an end.

The Ministry of Education Building (plates 1–6) attracted world-wide attention as the first public building clearly expressing the concepts of the modern achitectural movement. It was finished in 1943 at the time of the "obliteration of Baedeker" and of the mass slaughter with which mankind was preoccupied. The group of architects who worked on the design of this building, besides Lucio Costa and Niemeyer, included people whose subsequent careers produced some of the most worthy architectural achievements of our time. Jorge Moreira, as chief architect for the new campus of the National University of Brazil on Governador Island in the Guanabara Bay of Rio de Janeiro, was instrumental in designing the School of Architecture (among other faculty buildings) which embodies a thoroughly conceived program within the most severe, diagrammatic envelope emphasizing the values of the indispensable. Affonso Reidy is now known as the architect for the Modern Art Museum of Rio de Janeiro, for the "Pedregulho" low-cost housing complex and for a number of educational buildings.[17] The Ministry of Education Building consists of two major components: a low, two-story element with an east-west orientation, and a fourteen-story block facing north-south. The low part is designed to accommodate the functions associated with the heavy traffic of people: auditorium, exhibition hall, paymaster's facilities, information desk and main lobbies; the high part provides office space for the various departments of the Ministry, with the Minister's offices on the lowest level (33 feet above the ground) and recreational and dining facilities in the penthouse. The sunbreak forming an over-all pattern on the northern façade (plate 1) consists of a permanently fixed frame in the form of a honeycomb and of movable, adjustable louvers, painted light blue, whose angle can be regulated by a lever from inside the offices. The offices are provided with separate circulation for the visiting public and the staff. Low partitions within these offices combined with relatively high ceilings allow a continuous movement of air from north to south. The level of noise is low, owing perhaps to a minimum use of business machines. The long years spent on the study of this building and in the perfection of the final drawings are indicative of the responsibility felt by a design group fully aware that the Ministry of Education was a proving ground for the modern architectural movement in Brazil. The result justified the cautious effort. Actually the 1936 preliminary plans were subjected to the following revisions: the height of the stilts was more than doubled so as to open up the view of the garden and make the space lighter; the high block was moved from a street alignment, where it was to face another tall building across the street, to about the middle of the site; and the high block became wider to accommodate the elevator tower which was previously located in an extension.

This building served also as the first tangible application of a new concept which was emerging as "integration of the arts"—a haunting term at the present time.

Integration of the arts was to be the subject of innumerable meetings of art critics, aesthetic philosophers, financial and managerial executives of museums and all those who in our culture specialize in integration at large. Thus, we find the Social Utopias from Amaurot to Oneida followed by the Technological Utopias of not so long ago (sublimation through mechanical appliances) and now, by the Art Utopias —the ideal ground where all arts shall live together in harmony like monks or odalisques for the service of man. But modern man with his longings for eternity and with his seeking for a paradise is perplexed in the midst of history or torn between the absurd and the tragic. Are the tortuous ways that lead to his emotional life so easily accessible?

Looking now at the works of art which were placed about the Ministry of Education Building, we are less certain about their role than at the time of the building's inauguration; their rate of aging is somewhat faster than that of the supporting architecture. The healthy, gigantic couple ("Youth" by Bruno Giorgi) which stands on the ground and faces the southern façade of the building (the plain façade without the sunbreak) is reminiscent of the "Unafraid Workers" by unionized sculptors in the United States striving to express the moods of the late thirties.[18] The small robin ("Prometheus" by Jacques Lipchitz) appears uneasy in his temporary perch on the extrados of the auditorium. It seems that the works that survive are the mural of Candido Portinari in ceramic tile which underlines the new kind of betwixt-and-between space on the ground level (plate 6) and the lusty garden designed and planted by Burle-Marx.

After the early designs for the Ministry of Education Building, Niemeyer devoted himself to plastic research and to experimentation with a variety of forms corresponding to widely different architectural programs, as if the young architect wanted to submit himself to a number of difficult tests and watch the outcome of the challenge. By that time—at the outset of World War II—the modern architectural movement, perhaps through a meeting of minds, had reached a certain uniformity of expression and a certain virtuosity in the design of architectural elements and construction details. A faithful survey of this "new" architecture was made by Alfred Roth in 1939.[19] Out of twenty examples chosen as representative of the architectural movement in ten countries (with particular emphasis on Switzerland and Holland) and out of a variety of building types (from week-end houses to swimming-pool enclosures), clear trends could be detected: first, the diminished use of reinforced concrete as a structural, plastic medium and greater emphasis on dry assemblies of manufactured components; second, the further idealization of function as expressed in the large Headquarters for Social Security in Prague, the design of which is based entirely on filing systems and index-card sizes.

The departure of Niemeyer toward aesthetic preoccupations and away from the prevailing austerity and rigorous rationalization (any pursuit of the latter may have been handicapped by the low potential of a young building industry in Brazil) is seen clearly in his work in Pampulha. This work was instrumental in further strengthening his professional reputation but, in the light of his later architectural activities, in the breadth, scope and sheer number of the buildings that were to follow, Pampulha should be considered as a laboratory, a pilot experiment. It was then a newly developed residential suburb of Belo Horizonte with an artificial lake as its major feature. President Kubitschek of Brazil—then mayor of the city—commissioned Niemeyer to design a number of buildings which would enhance the community life of the suburb and provide additional recreational facilities for the people of Belo Horizonte, the capital of the State of Minas Gerais with fast-growing industrial areas. The buildings consist of a casino, a yacht club, a restaurant and a small church, all on the shores of the lake (figure 5); a hundred-room hotel for vacationers did not go beyond the planning stage. The casino rigidly follows a traditional program: a hall, restaurant, game room and theater, where people meet, dine, try their luck and/or watch a spectacle. As an architectural program this may represent a pure essence—the intangibles of a locus of pleasure—of that which previously had been expressed in the dream palaces of the Côte d'Azur and the grotesque constructions of other watering places throughout Europe. Modern architecture, until then concerned with the health, the rational comportment of man and his physiological needs—fresh air, sunshine and contact with nature—remained aloof from man's night life. It is true that in the early thirties Robert

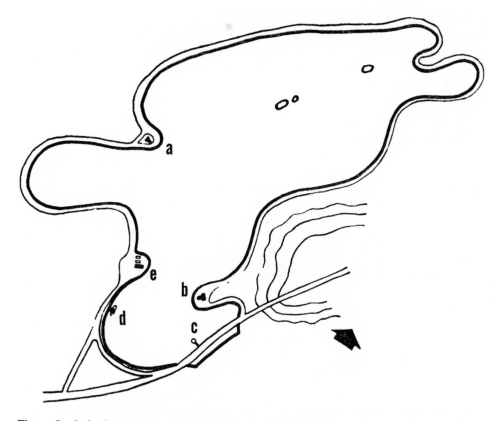

Figure 5. Lake Pampulha: a, Church of St. Francis of Assisi; b, Casino; c, Pier; d, "Baile" Restaurant; e, Yacht Club

Mallet-Stevens designed the casino of Saint-Jean-de-Luz, on the Gulf of Gascony, France, but this building was mainly to provide facilities for family sea-bathing.

Niemeyer approached the problem with a great deal of aplomb, and his design is for contemporary informality without a total loss of the grand manner (plate 131). The casino consists of a cubical building containing the main hall and game room, combined with an oval-shaped building for the restaurant and theater. Here, in the absence of functional data, lacking any programmatic restraint and with a circulation flow, the pattern of which was left entirely to his imagination, Niemeyer produced a rather sober building with severe contours, in which the play of the inner and outer spaces, the floating ramps, the contrasts in room heights and the absence of continuous visual barriers are the only elements of this "architecture of pleasure." Thus, the same plastic means which until then were applied to functional problems could also be used, with discretion of course, in buildings of marginal utility—buildings which, although they cannot be classified as "pleasure machines," should not be relegated to the treatment of county-fair tents. The acceptance of the non-functional as a legitimate architectural task marks a turning point in the modern architectural movement. By the 1950's the non-functional, the erratic and the irrational (in spite of the fact that surrealism has had very little influence on architecture so far[20]) became a welcome theme for some of our younger architects.

The yacht club (plates 132–134) which faces the casino across the bay is designed with a far more definite program: boat-house, lockers, first-aid station and, on the second floor, lounge and restaurant extending to an open terrace over the water. The lowest height of the roof (which has an inverted pitch) corresponds with the main division of the second floor. This is a small building planned with precision and economy of means. The outer shell and the interior spaces, which are enlivened by the rising heights of the ceilings and by the modulation of light through the changing patterns of the two tiers of vertical louvers (plate 132), provide a maximum visual impact. The restaurant "Baile" (plates 135–137) is practically a building without a building; a full moon upon which a half moon is superimposed forms the dining and service areas. An extension consisting of a non-building (plate 135), in counterplay to the contours of the shore, is the most important area of the restaurant and ends in a circular stage platform with a lily pond (an inlet) as the proscenium. The peristyle with unexpected, meandering directions, defining a landscape rather than a building function, appears here for the first time. Later it is to play an important role in grouping a number of differentiated buildings so as to unite them into a single organism, as in the São Paulo Exposition (plate 60). It is transformed, still later, into a system of platforms and ramps in the Place of the Three Powers, in Brasilia.

The small Church of Saint Francis of Assisi (plates 26–29) was the most difficult and controversial building of the group. The modern architectural movement, as has been said before, was being developed in pronounced materialistic directions within the dialectics of function and form and, further, with rationalizing activities borrowed from the natural sciences. (The deductive method had been officially accepted by the International Congresses for Modern Architecture in 1929 as the only possible way to obtain guiding principles.[21]) Thus, very few examples of contemporary religious architecture were then in existence. Frank Lloyd Wright had built the Unity Temple in 1904 at Oak Park, Illinois, but this building was rather "in the nature of the materials" than in the nature of architecture, at least as it was seen forty years later.[22] The Church of Our Lady of Raincy by Auguste Perret in 1924 was above all a brilliant research into the potentialities of reinforced concrete. Here many "firsts" were introduced: standardized molds, precast wall units for a free-standing enclosure and standardized structural elements (the nave and the bell tower are supported by the same type of columns from identical molds). This building, defined by a "continuous wall of light" and expressed in what was considered a humble material, was the first major departure from conventional church design. Yet, Perret's classical frame of mind confined him to symmetrical solutions and well-balanced façades. Le Corbusier said then that the façades would lead Perret to the French Institute but the cross section of the building would retard this event—such was the effect of the crystalline, dematerialized and all-of-the-spirit section of this building. Karl Moser's Church of Saint Anthony, built two years later (1926) in a conservative, middle-class district of Basel, is a larger structure also of exposed reinforced concrete. With more restraint in its concept than the Raincy Church, its outer columns are part of the exterior wall, a solution which Perret consciously avoided.[23] The Romanesque-inspired bell tower informally located outside the church to the right of the altar dominates the axis of the street; the vaulted concrete ceiling of the nave and the flat ceilings of the aisles, also of concrete, are covered by a traditional roof.[24] It could be said that Niemeyer's church retains both the homogeneous and somewhat fluid quality of Raincy and the independent treatment of the bell tower of Saint Anthony; but the section (closer in form to the hangars of Orly by Freyssinet in spite of the enormous difference in scale), the development of the interior volume and the applied polychromy on some of the exteriors place it quite apart from its predecessors.

The use of a single continuous structural element for walls and roof has an enormous appeal to the architect as having a very efficient unifying force and to the technologist as the only clear solution providing economy of means. This longing to obtain unity through method rather than conceptual effort is responsible during recent years for the great number of hyperbolic-paraboloid and spherical proposals for the solution of any one architectural problem as if, to use an expression of Henri Poincaré, man were a two-dimensional and pliable being.* As an over-all solution the big umbrella, which protects anything that happens to be under it, offers only quantitative differentiation: it could be any size. Paraboloid forms, the major focal theme at the Brussels Fair of 1958, have also become the protectors of the humble activities of the house—cooking and eating and bringing up children. The bird cage became a hangar, a shelter between flights.

Since its use in the Church of Saint Francis, this form has never been applied with so much discretion in regard to its over-all appearance and with so much concern over the enclosure it defines. The nave is of parabolic design on the plane of the cross section, approaching the form of a half a frustum of a cone in the longitudinal section (plate 28); the space of the altar is prescribed by a smaller parabolic form, and the same form is repeated three times on a still smaller scale and is used for the sacristy and the vestry. Light entering the narthex, is modulated by vertical

* In such an instance man could make the fullest use of curved surfaces.

23

louvers on the front façade. Beyond, the primary lighting coming from above falls just before the altar, separating it from the worshippers. The rear façade is a ceramic tile mural by Candido Portinari[25] depicting scenes from the life of Saint Francis. These scenes appear on an over-all tile pattern of birds and fishes—the friends of the Saint (plate 29). The church, surrounded by flora arranged by Burle-Marx, presents a rather modest and inviting appearance, closer to the humility that Saint Francis suggests than to the celebration of the "Glory of God" which was the role of the Gothic cathedral. However, reaction provoked by the design was violent and prolonged; one mayor insisted on its demolition and replacement by a replica from the colonial town of Ouro Preto. A miscellany of furnishings was introduced so as to destroy the visual order of the interior. The Office of National Artistic Patrimony had to intervene and maintenance of the church now remains the responsibility of that organization.

The small number of buildings around the shores of Lake Pampulha, although visible to anyone standing on any point of the shore, do not form a coherent group. They were not meant to influence visually or to complement each other. If they had been conceived as an entity, a transmutation of forms would have been inevitable, sacrificing the absolute independence with which every building had been developed; Niemeyer would have lost all the worth of the experiment which—as his later buildings proved—demonstrated his creative potential. Lucio Costa, with characteristic restraint, was then justified in saying: "Niemeyer, by giving to basic architectural forms a new and surprising meaning, created variations and new solutions with local patterns which have a grace and a subtlety until then unknown to modern architecture"; and Le Corbusier: ". . . you know how to give full freedom to the discoveries of modern architecture."

"There is a marvellous spring dispersed among the seasons"

—RENÉ CHAR

3. THE CASE FOR A LYRICAL ARCHITECTURE

ACADEMIC ARCHITECTURE, that is to say architecture inspired by the composite glories of the past, is now generally abandoned. This is partly the consequence of the "Crusade"[26] of Le Corbusier, but it is most certainly the result of the demands of an economic determinism which is in force today and which is incompatible with any kind of forms, old or new. The building now tends to reflect the nature of the organization of which it is the instrument, and the nature of the organization is statistical and extensible. Thus, during the second part of this century the prevailing architectural modus is a quantitative one; it corresponds with the forces directed toward the depersonalization of the individual, toward the eventual alienation of the individual from himself in his attempt to "make" history or to live in it; it is in accordance with the prophecies of the romantic philosophers of a hundred and fifty years ago. A building becomes "extensible" with relation to its size, "flexible" with relation to its function—a visual and factual probability. Its form derives from statistical activities, from data abstracted from topical realities and local conditions; its height and depth are tabulated. The impact of architect-committee and client-committee creates solutions within a situation of chance—"chance being the irrational meeting of independent causal series," to quote Cournot, the father of modern probabilism. Two basic *modi operandi* are in evidence. One, mention of which was made earlier, is to be found in the parabolic or spherical proposals for all types of architectural spaces—for generalized architectural space. Buckminster Fuller also proposes the substitution of vectorial coordinates for the humble, inert coordinates of Euclidian space; this substitution will put an end to the use of numbers, proportional ratios, rhythms—all the invariables which have appeared in architectural design during some milennia—and will establish, thus, a truly new era. The other is the application of the "cold skin" as a means of stretching and covering any statistical volume with a pattern simulating graph paper; this is found suitable for small structures and "mile-high" buildings. Both methods imply that function-form dialectics are now bypassed and the gates are open for the neutral kingdom of Heidegger. In order to eliminate the conflict diagnosed by Hegel between duration (man) and cycles (nature), K. Lönberg-Holm and to a lesser extent Frederick Kiesler propose duration cycles to replace natural cycles; "research, production, consumption and elimination" correspond *grosso modo* to spring, summer, autumn and winter, but each with a variable, asymptotic span of time and without the notion of regeneration.[27]

The same redirections can be seen clearly in an activity which by its nature is not expected to be susceptible to the immediate influences of changing world attitudes. It is at the same time that we have in painting the enormous, quasi-anonymous landscapes of the Tohu and the Bohu, of the original chaos in front of which a public waits patiently for the event of the Creation, the six days that shaped the world. Called sometimes the "other art," painting is directed towards the origins before the origins, and to the things before the beginnings for an answer, perhaps to the probable and to the frame of history.[28] Painters like Fernand Léger—he died in 1955—appear now unbelievably archaic; his work is like fairy tales, tournaments of brave worker-knights and Elysian sites of machine tools.

While architecture built "castles in Spain" before the First World War, after the Second World War it concerned itself entirely with the dehumanization of space. In this activity architecture became the instrument of the powerful forces now in evidence. To counter this movement, to rediscover man, there is no crusade; there is more silence than protest. But nevertheless architecture continues to flower; it is to be found in no longer so distant places as Chandigarh in India and Brasilia in Brazil among others and, perhaps, in more examples than the 1920's have produced, but not so many as is often thought. Niemeyer continued his work with great fortitude, seemingly oblivious to the grave changes in the architectural climate. Indulging in the ineffable delight of designing buildings, in the creative process which cannot be subjected to quantitative analysis but lives in the imagining faculties, he produced a wealth of types, sizes and kinds of architectural spaces, all of which retain certain common characteristics. It can be said—and this should be considered his greatest asset—that there is no new departure, no abrupt turn to be traced in his work. The same characteristics that existed in his early work became even more prominent in the multiplicity of his later designs. In small, large or enormous buildings; whether the usual program as in dwelling blocks, or unique as in a presidential "palace"; whether designing for exacting functions as in a museum, or creating pure structural phantasy as in a youth club, we see the same intent: the transformation of architecture into a joyous event.

This transformation is not based on a simple, mechanical activity nor on an act of will; it is certainly not the result of the impulse of a talent. The slow, gradual subordination of given realities (the seemingly irreconcilable arbitrary realities of program, materials and budget) to a stronger reality of form and content, to that particular reality which is the "work" with a face and identity all its own, is not accomplished by analytical and rational operations, nor by the mediation of a system under the guidance of a given methodology. Active imagination—imagination in action with its power to associate images with a freedom, order and logic which are of its nature, continuously nourished by an inexhaustible unconscious—can alone precipitate this act of transformation ("of" a reality "to" the reality) which has the appearance of the miraculous. Then, buildings acquire their own destiny; the shape they prescribe comes to life; and conflicts between container and content fade away. The event of such a new reality is always a surprising one, a welcome surprise: an image that in its turn stimulates the imagining faculties and becomes the source of a still newer series of images within man's emotional being.

The effects of this multiple imagery of Niemeyer can be seen in projects of similar content. In the "Julia Kubitschek" grammar school in Diamantina (plates 39–42) (named after the mother of the President who taught school for forty years in this small mountainous center of Minas Gerais), the classrooms, all on the second floor, float over shaded grounds. The building is placed lightly on a gentle slope and its profile is turned toward the light and the distant horizons. A ramp with a low incline slows the transition between floors. In the absence of any constraint, of any noticeable structural tour-de-force (all projections are an integral part of the main body) or of any unexpected, added volumes, one is amazed with the simple, elementary aspect of the undertaking and becomes oblivious to the pre-existence of a program. The much larger secondary school in Belo Horizonte (plates 43–47) is, on the contrary, developed on the basis of co-existence of diversified elements within the unity of the multiple. The classrooms again float over the site, but the auditorium—a kind of Noah's ark of a twice-folded slab—is lightly, almost temporarily placed on the ground. A low, one-story wing extends at a right angle from the classroom building and an equally low structure for student activities stands independently at the rear. Here the long and the short, the regular rectangular form and the invented one, the free standing and the attached, the suspended and the reclining, the forefront and the front, the rear and the postrear, all on flat ground but high above the street level, make an intensive entity. Only the site with its simple pattern of gravel and green-ground cover provides the unifying element. But the same serenity as in the previous school can be noticed here, the result of an ease by which programmatic demands are intensified, translated into compact forms or dispersed. The fact that the shape of the auditorium resulted from the placement of a minimum enclosure around a speaker and a seated group, is of less importance than the intent to mold space into contrasting or complementary forms and, within the existing possibilities of a program, to be quiet and lively at the same time.

Also, in his recent design of three religious buildings, images rather than concepts become evident. Each of them, designed almost consecutively between 1957 and 1959, represents a different religious moment. The small presidential chapel in Brasilia (plates 30–32) is close in feeling to a crypt—to a place of retirement for spiritual concentration. The plan consists of two interlocking half-circles of different radii but in elevation the form is a continuous helicoid. The dominant element here is the event of light; one enters in darkness and, with a turn to the right, faces the altar, which is brightly lit from an invisible daylight source.

The Chapel of Our Lady of Fatima (plate 33) is a larger structure for parochial services. Situated on a level site, the building is a tent with the roof as the dominant element. The spiritual use of the tent is, of course, an extension of the temporal shelter with its suggestion of informal and inviting hospitality. The roof suspended loosely on three points rises higher at the apex (over the entrance) and is lowered at the base of the triangle. The enclosing wall, almost uninterrupted, is approximately a U shape opening outwards at the entrance; the blue azulejos which cover the wall from floor to ceiling contribute to the visual effacement of the wall and further emphasize the importance of the roof. On the inner side of the wall a fresco by Alfredo Volpi, predominantly blue with sparingly arranged geometric patterns, enhances the tent image with its continuity. The design of the Cathedral of Brasilia, now under construction, is based on the centripetal nature of the sacred space. The sacred pole, the sacred tree and the sacred mountain have been religious symbols or realities since prehistory and, according to Mircea Eliade, are the only physical dimension of sacred space.[29] Here, however, the pole is a cone of light to which another dimension has been added, that of ascension. The Cathedral (plates 37, 38) is circular in plan with a diameter approximating 232 feet; its volume is defined by twenty-one buttresses converging toward the top, opening out again and finally united by a halo-like ring. The height enclosed is over 131 feet. The circular pattern is maintained by locating sacristy, baptistry, vestry and offices outside the main building, while thirteen chapels are placed around the periphery of the main floor which is about ten feet below ground level. The worshipers enter through an underground passage being thus subjected to the full impact of the cone of light. This way of entering the Cathedral eliminates the need for axial gates which might have interrupted the continuous enclosing form.

A house, in its double role of a shelter and of a center where we dream, offers the most fecund suggestions for a multitude of interpretations in depth and form. The Cavanelas house in Pedro do Rio (plates 78–82) is situated on the bottom of

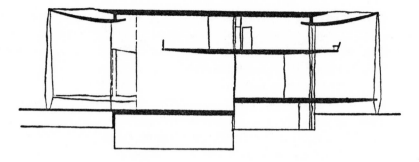

Figure 6. Palace of the Dawn, Brasilia, 1959. Section

an alluvial valley which has been drained and landscaped in its entirety. Although this house is designed as an open tent, privacy is assured by the surrounding hills. Under the suspended roof the humble functions of a dwelling occupy but a small part of the total floor area while the rest seems to remain a part of the valley. The building here is a minimum statement; even the masonry piers at the corners and some free standing walls belong more to the landscape than to the house—a house which was conceived to mark, with a great subtlety, a temporal passage. The private life of a president of a republic is a public one while the life of a monarch is witnessed only by the court. Thus, the presidential residence (plates 83–90) is an open one, a glass cage inviting, so to speak, the scrutiny of the citizenry. Since the content must, of necessity, be influenced by this reality, the private quarters of the family are relatively small. Much of the space is given to elements which are necessary to stage and enliven a state event: halls interlocking or continuing on different levels, ramps and loops permitting the return to the same points, terraces resting on the ground or suspended in mid-height. Furthermore, mirrored surfaces produce an endless mirage and break all visual boundaries with multiple reflections. A small amount of privacy is suggested by the fact that the "palace" is enclosed by a light screen consisting of twenty-two caryatids (and a half-one on each of the four corners). Closer to the frontal picture of a swan than to a maid of Athens, the caryatids are in harmony with the surrounding body of still water from which they emerge and which is conducive to aquatic images. The main floor is raised on a level with the outdoor terraces, while the entrance hall remains a continuation of the ground level. This allows a triple variation in height: single, double and one plus (figure 6). Toward the right of the entrance are two figures by the sculptor Ceshiatti which provide a massive foil for the lightness of architecture, a contrast which Niemeyer often employs. The lighter, open sculpture by Maria Martins is placed against a distant horizon at the end of the rear terrace (plate 84). Some of the interior walls are covered with ceramic tiles, but here the azulejo, the "bluish one," has a warm, golden sheen.

The Modern Art Museum in Carácas, Venezuela (plates 51–56), is a building intended to be a landmark; it contrasts the activities in a continuous becoming which are related to this type of museum with a rigid, finite form, with all the permanence that such a form may suggest. Thus, an activity without foreseen limits is not further complicated by endless architectural forms, with an architecture also in becoming. The inverted pyramid or, rather, the frustum of an inverted pentahedron with faces of reinforced concrete slabs and floors acting as ties in two directions at a right angle to each other, is a simple structural form (which however should not be applied to every kind of architectural problem). The large horizontal area on the top provides maximum daylight illumination—a giant skylight. To take advantage of this, the two upper floors—a complete floor and a mezzanine directly above it in the shape of a bird in flight—are given over to exhibition space; as the mezzanine occupies but a fraction of the total area, daylight penetrates large parts of the floor below. To avoid glare a special horizontal sunbreak was devised. Two narrow strips of paved areas on the roof interrupt the sunbreak and provide facilities for outdoor sculpture exhibitions. There is space for storage and shops under the large platform upon which the pyramid rests. An auditorium level with the ground accommodates four hundred people, and on the level directly above are located the main foyer, reception desk and offices. Niemeyer considers this building as marking an important stage of his work: a discipline toward minimum means of expression—the translation of a program, no matter how complicated it may be, into an elementary form. (A somewhat similar result had been obtained earlier by the overwhelming development of the non-operational spaces of his buildings, through expansion rather than through contraction. The effect of a pronounced aspect of dematerialization in his buildings could be directly attributed to the apparent immensity of those areas in contrast to the calculated and precision-planned functional parts.) Elementary forms and familiar forms require a particularly sensitive handling of scale, a delicate but exacting dimensioning if they are to acquire an identity and become a source of imagery and not remain an abstract and inert formula of space. According to Niemeyer the plastic possibilities explored in the Modern Art Museum in Carácas had a major influence on his later work in Brasilia.

As chief architect for Novacap, Niemeyer is responsible for the design of all the important federal buildings of the new capital of Brazil, including the Cathedral, the general hospital and one housing super-block (plates 109–112) of four hundred and forty-four dwelling units with their related facilities: school, market, motion picture theater and church (plates 33–36). The presidential palace (Palacio da Alvorada, Palace of the Dawn) and a three-hundred-room hotel (plates 120–126) were designed earlier, before the establishment of the city's general plan, and are situated on peripheral grounds. Niemeyer, with the assistance of about sixty young architects, whose complete devotion to their calling should not be underestimated, was able to conceive, develop and produce final drawings of those buildings within a span of less than two years. This presupposes a state of unheard-of euphoria—even in the presence of a self-stimulating activity—to which we have not been accustomed since the time of the High Renaissance. For this enormous task he had the generous assistance of Lucio Costa, the Chief Planning Officer, and of Joaquim Cardozo,[30] Chief Structural Engineer. Such convergence of talent enjoying the unqualified trust of temporal power created, in the absence of clear historical precedents, a sense of bewilderment among many people and shocked the professionals. It is true that in 1631 Cardinal Richelieu commissioned Jacques Lemercier to build on the Loire a town which would bear the Cardinal's name. In fulfilling this assignment Lemercier exhibited a considerable mastery of design but the town of Richelieu was a very small enterprise. We have to go beyond our era, into the deep shadows of history to find undertakings similar to Brasilia, but this is hardly the place to discuss this subject in its proper depth and with its many aspects.

If the design of every major government building had been left to individual architects subject only to the approval of a committee—as is so often the practice today—the resulting effect would have been similar to a world's fair where every country and every industry erects a pavilion competing in ostentation. In fairs, however, such an activity is tolerated, if not encouraged, by the non-permanent life of its architecture and by an inherent indifference toward the grouping of temporary buildings. It is true that city spaces, that is to say spaces which come into existence by virtue of the presence of buildings, acquire qualities quite independent of those of the surrounding buildings which serve to shape these open spaces. But it is hard to believe that architectural anarchy could contribute to a fundamental definition of the voids which are the urban spaces and which are not to be confused with the quaint aspects of small market corners and with the occasional creation of vistas. Thus, the mechanics of modern democracy with its safeguards and its promises is presented to the citizens of Brasilia in tangible and finite visual form: the *triangle* of the Three Powers, a shape that is the most stable and self-balanced of all shapes.[31] This is quite a new concept for a symbol, a "monument"—if such a term should be used. In the past, political personages were honored with elaborate shrines in the same way as successful generals. Commemoration, however, is not a symbol but remains informative and didactic and very rarely can become the source of imagery.

The Congress Building is at the apex of the Triangle (at the other points are the Supreme Court and the Executive House) (plates 19–25); as the seat of the Senate and of the House of Representatives it offers, and justly, the most dynamic form of the group. One half-sphere houses the Senate. A larger but inverted half-sphere encloses the Assembly. Both rest on a simple platform under which an elaborate circulation system separates the movement of legislators, staff, press and public—an enormous *pas-perdus*. In the foreground, between the two half-spheres, rises a tall building (plate 24), the only one in the Triangle, surrounded by a gigantic reflecting pool. This building, accommodating the offices of both legislative bodies in the twenty-five stories above the platform and three stories below, is shaped like an H both in plan and in elevation. The horizontal line of the H occurs on the eleventh, twelfth and thirteenth floors, leaving the impression that there are two independent buildings below and two above the mid-height. Behind the Congress Building lies the City of Brasilia on a gentle, fan-like rise of the grounds.

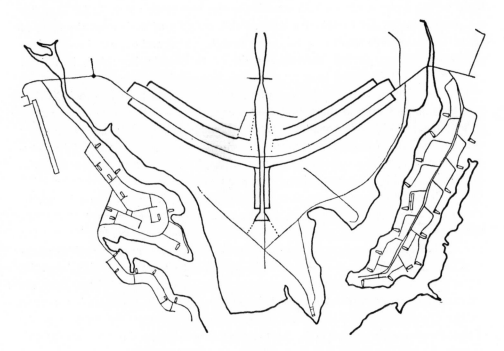

Figure 7.   Plan of Brasilia by Lucio Costa, 1957

The Notes to the Text begin on page 113.

1. Ministry of Education and Culture, Rio de Janeiro, 1937-43. Façade, with brise-soleil.

2. Ministry of Education. Northern façade with auditorium in the foreground.

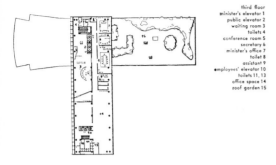

third floor
minister's elevator 1
public elevator 2
waiting room 3
toilets 4
conference room 5
secretary 6
minister's office 7
toilet 8
assistant 9
employees' elevator 10
toilets 11, 13
office space 14
roof garden 15

3. Ministry of Education. Third floor plan.

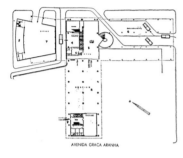

ground floor
2 portico
3 public hall
4 minister's entrance
5 information desk
6 parking
7 garage
8 machinery
9, 10 employees' entrance and hall

AVENIDA GRACA ARANHA

4. Ministry of Education. Ground floor plan.

5. Ministry of Education. Brise-soleil.

6. Ministry of Education. "Azulejo" (ceramic tile) mural by Candido Portinari.

7. Headquarters for the Boavista Bank, Rio de Janeiro, 1946. Southern façade.

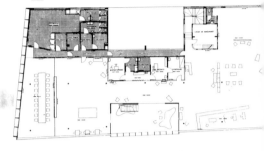

8. Boavista Bank. Typical floor plan.

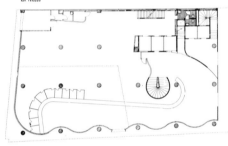

9. Boavista Bank. Ground floor plan.

10. Boavista Bank. Interior detail.

11. Boavista Bank, Brise-soleil (opposite page)

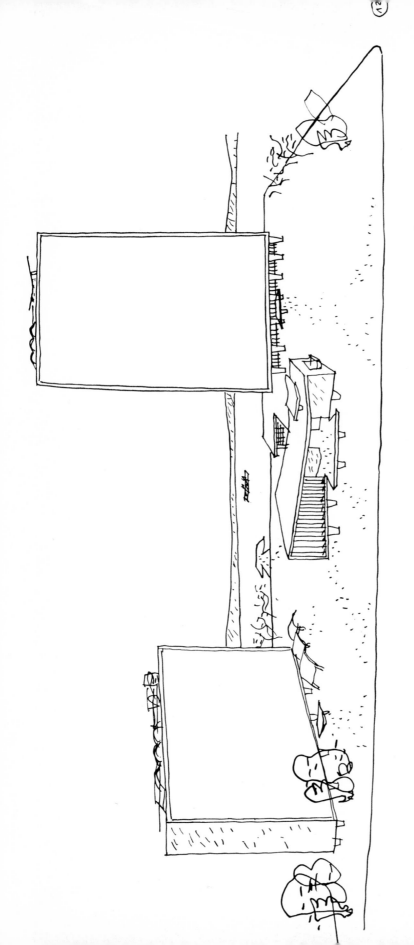

"23 - 32 K"

12. "Scheme 32" for the United Nations Headquarters, New York, 1947.

13. "Scheme 32". Model.

14. Montreal Building, São Paulo, 1950.

15. Montreal Building. Model.

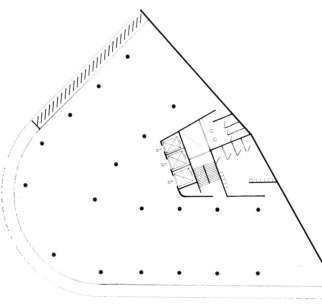

16. Montreal Building. Typical floor plan.

18. Getulio Vargas Foundation. Model.

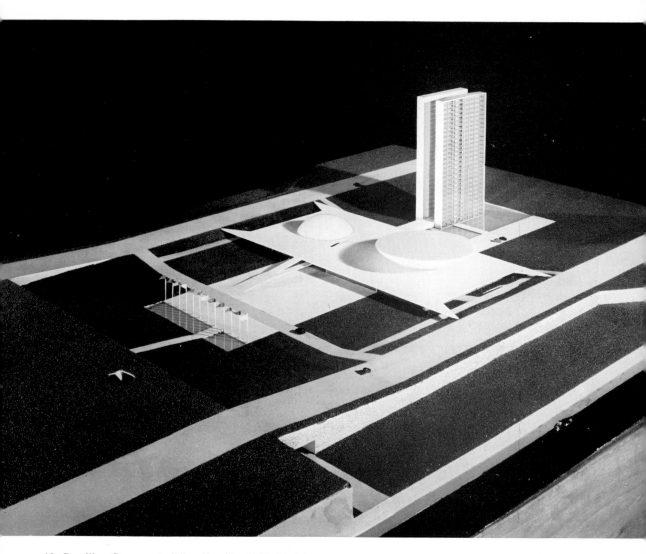

19. Brazilian Congress Building, Brasilia, 1958. Model.

20. Congress Building. Under construction.

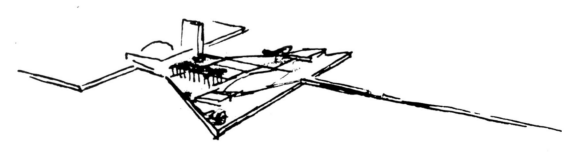

21. Congress Building. Sketch by Lucio Costa from his pilot plan for Brasilia, 1957.

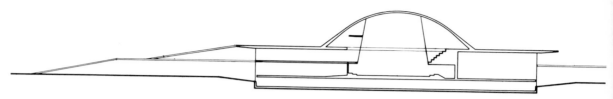

22. Congress Building. Section through Senate Chamber.

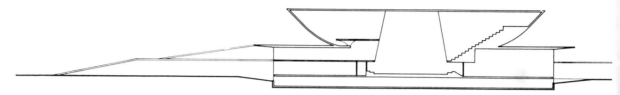

23. Congress Building. Section through House of Representatives.

24. Congress Building. Under construction.

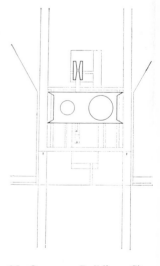

25. Congress Building. Site plan.

26. Church of Saint Francis of Assisi, Pampulha, Belo Horizonte, State of Minas Gerais, 1943.

27. Saint Francis of Assisi. Side view.

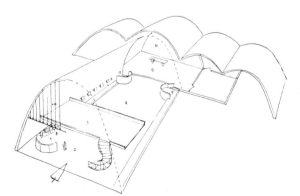

28. Saint Francis of Assisi. Isometric drawing.

29. Saint Francis of Assisi. Rear view, azulejo mural by Candido Portinari depicting the life of Saint Francis.

30. Presidential Chapel, Brasilia, 1958.

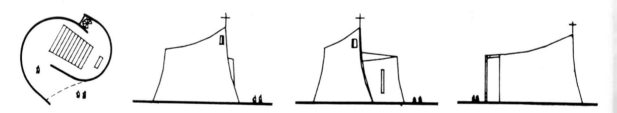

31. Presidential Chapel. Plan, elevations.

32. Presidential Chapel. Interior.

33. Chapel of Our Lady of Fatima, Brasilia, 1959.

34. Our Lady of Fatima. Interior.

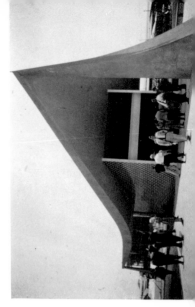

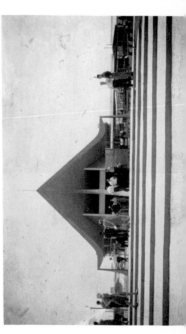

35, 36. Our Lady of Fatima. Exteriors.

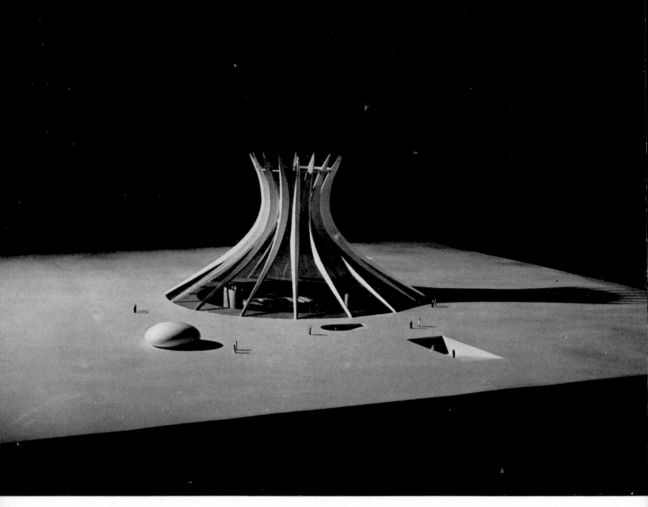

37. Cathedral, Brasilia, 1959. Model.

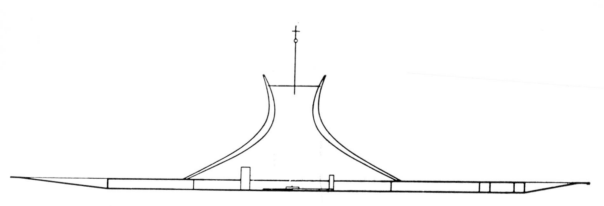

38. Cathedral. Section.

39. Julia Kubitschek Elementary School, Diamantina, State of Minas Gerais, 1951. Side and rear view.

40. Julia Kubitschek School. Front view.

48. Public Library, Belo Horizonte, State of Minas Gerais, 1955. Model.

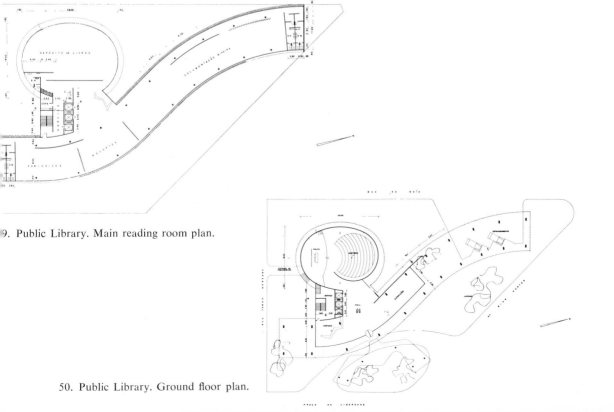

9. Public Library. Main reading room plan.

50. Public Library. Ground floor plan.

51. Modern Art Museum, Carácas, Venezuela, 1955. Model.

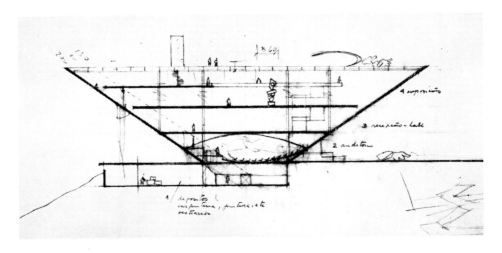

52. Modern Art Museum. Section.

53. Modern Art Museum. View of model from above.

54. Modern Art Museum. View of model showing ramp.

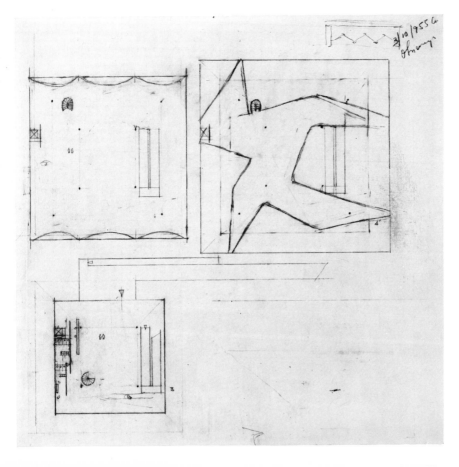

55. Modern Art Museum. Plans at the entrance level, main exhibition hall and mezzanine.

56. Modern Art Museum. Model.

57. Brazilian Pavilion for the New York World's Fair, New York, 1939.

58. Brazilian Pavilion. View from the lily pond.

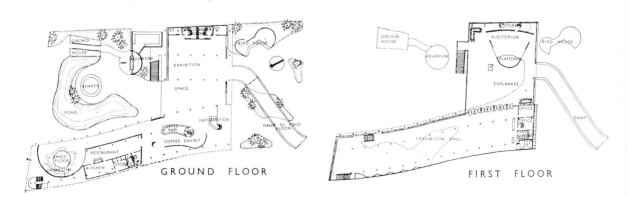

GROUND FLOOR

FIRST FLOOR

59. Brazilion Pavilion. Plan.

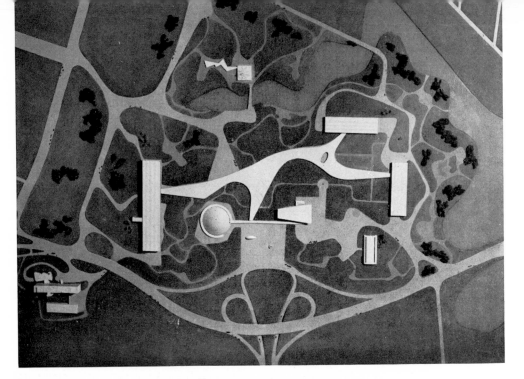

60. IV Centenary Exposition of São Paulo, São Paulo, 1954. General plan.

61. IV Centenary Exposition, Palace of Nations. Northwest façade.

62. IV Centenary Exposition, Palace of Agriculture. "Stilts."

63. IV Centenary Exposition. Aerial view.

64. IV Centenary Exposition, Palace of Industry. Access ramp.

65. Maternity Clinic, Rio de Janeiro, 1937. (The earliest building of the architect.)

66. Maternity Clinic. Ground floor plan.

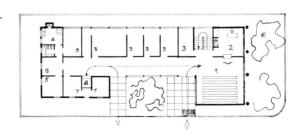

67. "Sul America" Hospital, Rio de Janeiro, 1952. Model, façade facing the lake.

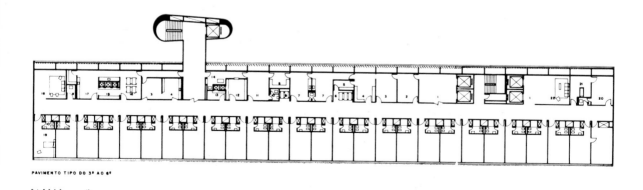

PAVIMENTO TIPO DO 3º AO 6º

68. "Sul America" Hospital. Nursing units, typical floor plan.

69. "Sul America" Hospital. Detail of the street façade under construction.

70. Week-end house of the architect, Mendes, 1949

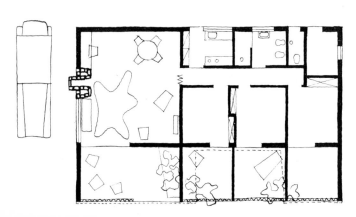

71. Week-end house. Plan.

72. House of the architect, Rio de Janeiro, 1953.

73. House of the architect. View toward access road.

74. House of the architect. Living room seen from dining corner.

75. House of the architect. Dining corner.

76. House of the architect. Exterior.

77. House of the architect. Main floor plan.

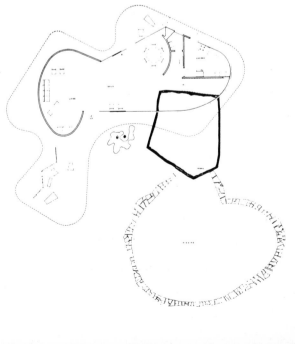

78. Cavanelas House, Pedro de Rio, 1954.

79. Cavanelas House. Section.

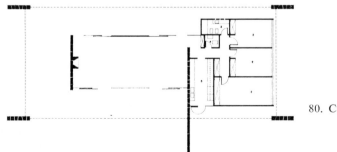

80. Cavanelas House. Plan.

81. Cavanelas House. Side view.

82. Cavanelas House. Formal garden by Roberto Burle-Marx.

83. Palace of the Dawn (Palacio da Alvorada), Brasilia, 1959. The official presidential residence.

84. Palace of the Dawn. Rear terrace with sculpture by Maria Martins.

85. Palace of the Dawn.

86. Palace of the Dawn. Entrance lobby seen from the mezzanine.

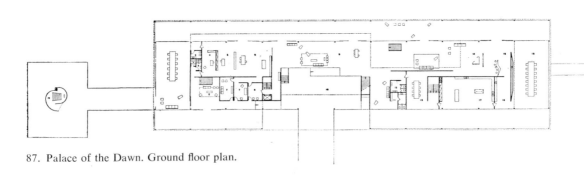

87. Palace of the Dawn. Ground floor plan.

88. Palace of the Dawn. Balcony accessible from the private quarters.

89. Palace of the Dawn. Bathroom.

90. Palace of the Dawn. Entrance lobby.

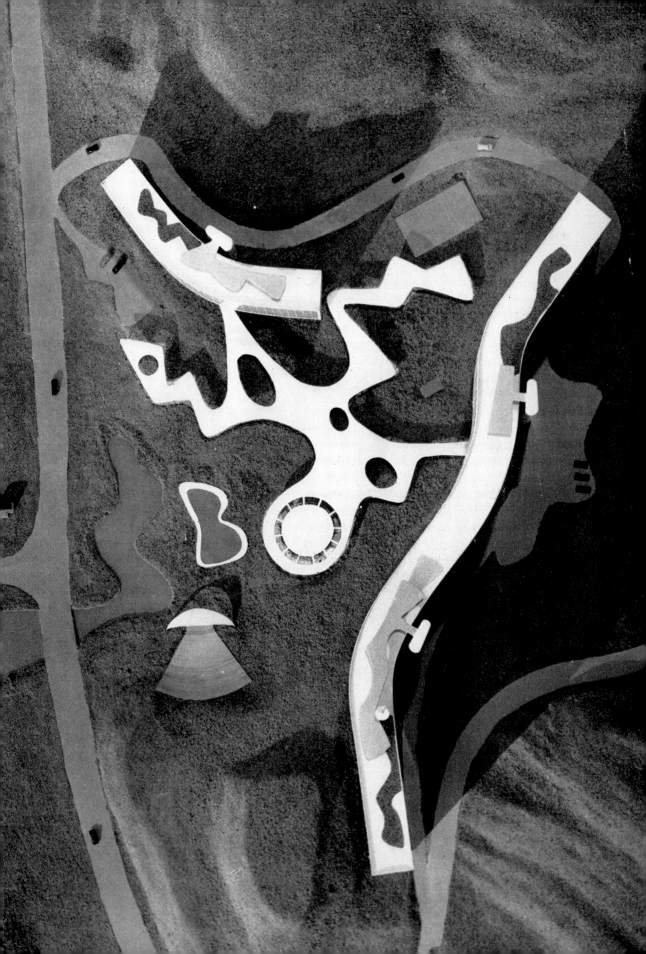

91. Residential Blocks, Petropolis, 1953. Air view of model (opposite page).

92. Petropolis. Model, view of the major and minor blocks.

93. Petropolis. Elevation. (Each apartment has two exposures and is on two levels.)

94. "Kubitschek Complex," Belo Horizonte, State of Minas Gerais, 1951. Model.

95. Kubitschek Complex. Construction view of elevator tower (opposite page).

96. Kubitschek Complex. Detail of the "stilt" under the main building.

105. Air Center Housing. View from corridor.

106. Air Center Housing. View from rear.

107. Row Houses, Brasilia, 1958. A dwelling unit.

108. Row Houses. Air view.

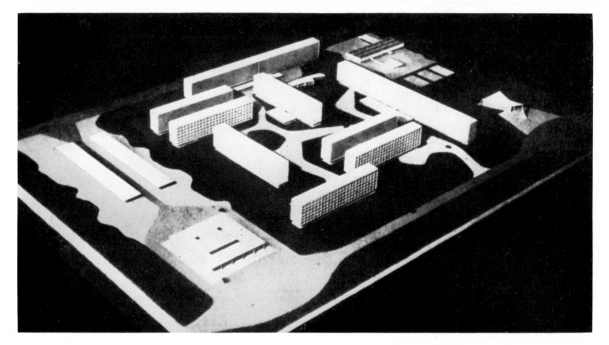

109. Residential Blocks, Brasilia, 1958. Model.

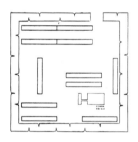

110. Residential
Blocks. Plan.

111. Residential Blocks,
Brasilia, 1959. Apart-
ment house unit.

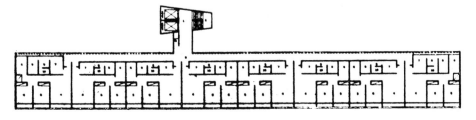

112. Residential Blocks.
Typical floor plan.

113. Hotel, Diamantina, State of Minas Gerais, 1951.

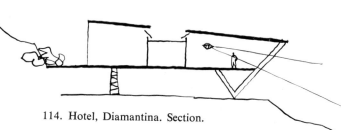

114. Hotel, Diamantina. Section.

115. Hotel, Diamantina. View of the hotel (upper right) from the town.

116. Hotel, Diamantina. Typical guest room floor plan.

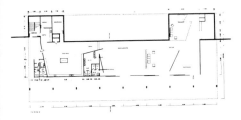

117. Hotel, Diamantina. Ground floor plan.

118. Hotel, Diamantina. Main terrace.

119. Hotel, Diamantina. Staircase.

120. Hotel, Brasilia, 1958. View of the guest room block showing corridor façade.

121. Hotel, Brasilia. Front façade.

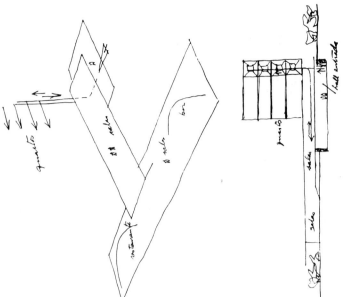

122. Hotel, Brasilia. Diagram of the distribution of functions.

123. Hotel, Brasilia. View of lounge toward dining room.

124. Hotel, Brasilia. Entrance hall.

125. Hotel, Brasilia. View of lounge toward the bar.

126. Hotel, Brasilia. Azulejos (opposite page).

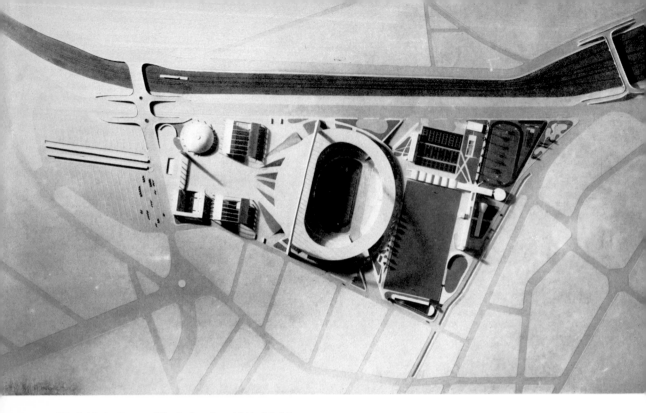

127. Athletic Center, Rio de Janeiro, 1941. Model.

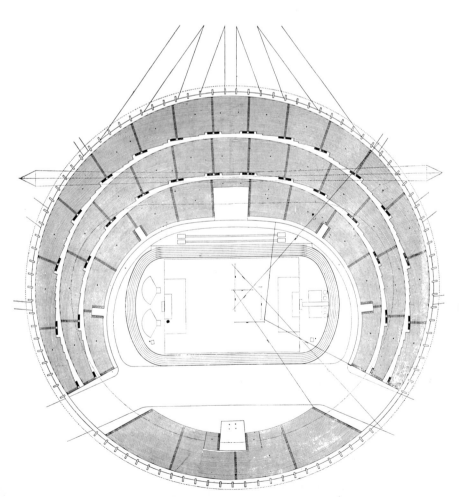

128. Athletic Center. Plan of main stadium.

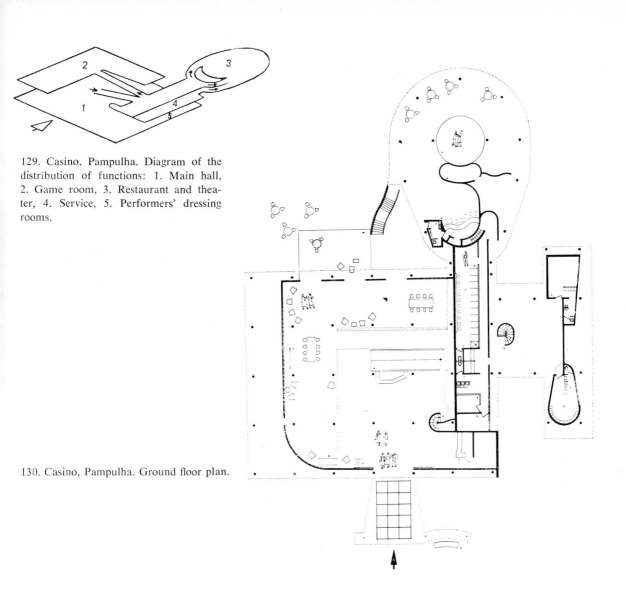

129. Casino, Pampulha. Diagram of the distribution of functions: 1. Main hall, 2. Game room, 3. Restaurant and theater, 4. Service, 5. Performers' dressing rooms.

130. Casino, Pampulha. Ground floor plan.

131. Casino, Pampulha, Belo Horizonte, State of Minas Gerais, 1942. Façade entrance.

132. Yacht Club, Pampulha, 1942. Main façade.

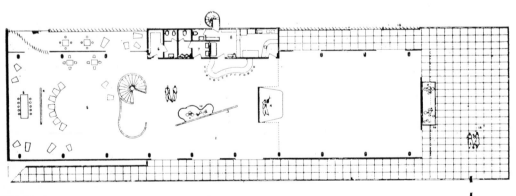

133. Yacht Club, Pampulha. Second floor plan.

134. Yacht Club, Pampulha. Detail of brise-soleil (opposite pag

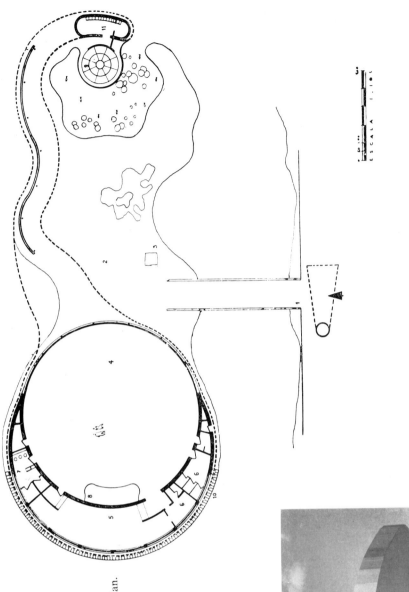

136. Restaurant, Pampulha. Plan.

137. Restaurant, Pampulha.

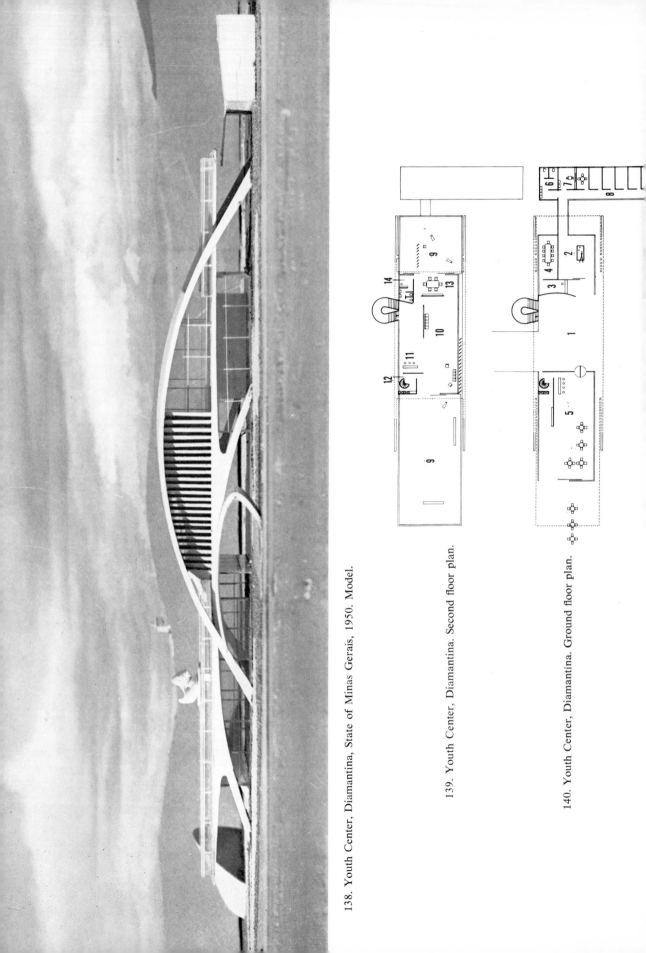

138. Youth Center, Diamantina, State of Minas Gerais, 1950. Model.

139. Youth Center, Diamantina. Second floor plan.

140. Youth Center, Diamantina. Ground floor plan.

141. Youth Center, Diamantina. Construction detail.

142. Youth Center, Diamantina. construction detail.

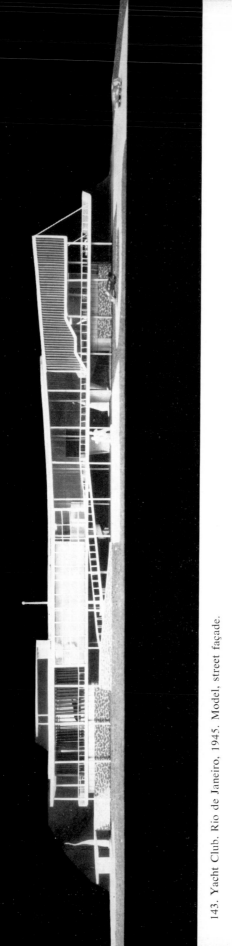

143. Yacht Club. Rio de Janeiro, 1945. Model, street façade.

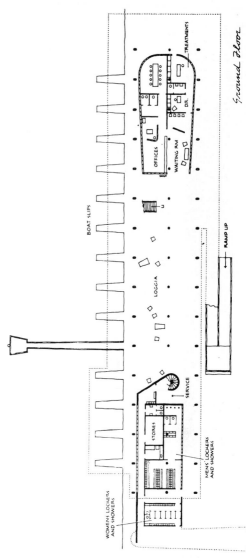

Ground Floor

BOAT SLIPS

OFFICES

WAITING RM.

DR.

TREATMENTS

LOGGIA

RAMP UP

SERVICE

STORES

MEN'S LOCKERS AND SHOWERS

WOMEN'S LOCKERS AND SHOWERS

144. Yacht Club, Rio de Janeiro. Ground floor plan.

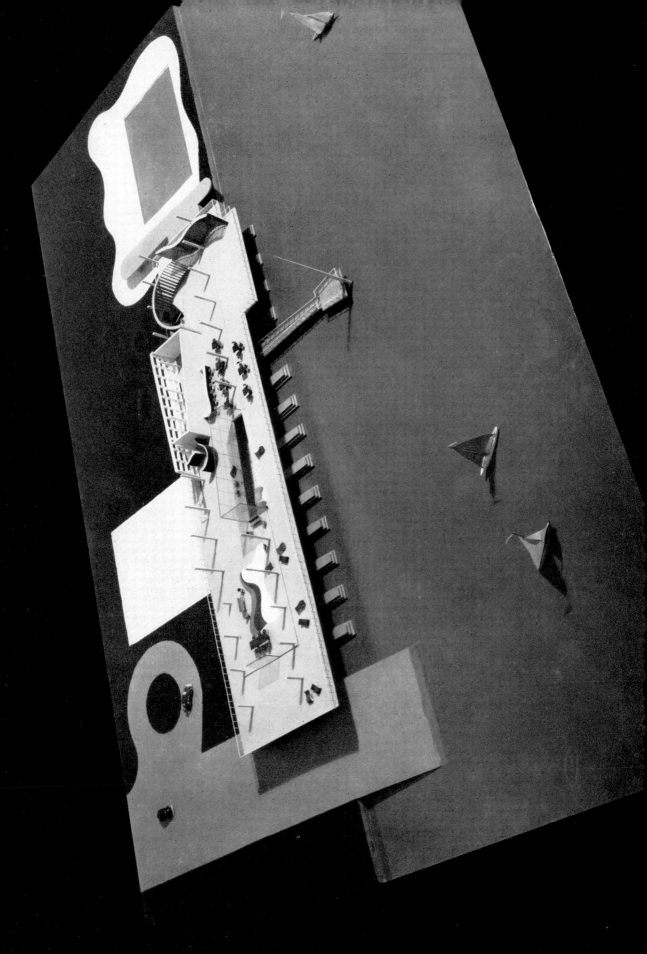

146. Stage setting by Niemeyer for "Black Orpheus", a lyrical drama by Vinicio Moraes, Rio de Janeiro, Municipal Opera House.

NOTES

1. See the second edition of *L'Envers et l'Endroit,* Gallimard, Paris, 1958; for other comments on the "happy climate" see also Camus' *Noces,* 1947 and *L'Ete,* 1954, by the same publisher.

2. Paul Valéry in his only essay on architecture, *Eupalinos ou l'Architecte,* Gallimard, Paris, 1924, comments on the given and the offered in the concept of a building.

3. François Lenormant, *La Grande Grèce,* A. Lévy, Paris, 1881-84.

4. The late professor and political figure of the Weimar Republic in his "Die Protestantische Ethik und der Geist des Kapitalismus" presented capitalism as the logical development of Calvinism; he cited also a passage from Wesley: "Religion engenders necessarily the spirit of work and the spirit of economy which cannot produce but wealth."

5. See Giuseppe Cocchiara, *Il Mito del Buon Selvaggio,* G. d'Anna, Messina, 1948, and Mircea Eliade, *Mythes, Rêves et Mystères,* Gallimard, Paris, 1957.

6. For social aspects of Brazil see Gilberto de Mello Freyre, *The Masters and the Slaves,* Knopf, New York, 1946; *New World in the Tropics,* Knopf, New York, 1959; also *Brazil: an Interpretation,* Knopf, New York, 1945, the latter a series of lectures delivered at the University of Indiana.

7. A friendly, informal surname for a native of the city of Rio de Janeiro; "Fluminense" is used for an inhabitant of the State of Rio de Janeiro.

8. Alberto Sartoris in his *Gli Elementi dell'Architettura Funzionale.* Ulrico Hoepli, Milan, 1932, used this term as synonymous with rational. Within the decade that followed, the term was used to designate a strictly materialistic approach to architecture—such is the destiny of words!

9. In the first book of the "Collection de l'Esprit Nouveau" by Le Corbusier (*Towards a New Architecture,* Crès et Cie, Paris, 1923) the title of the last chapter is "Architecture or Revolution."

10. The memoirs of Le Corbusier on his first trip to South America are in his book *Précisions sur l'Etat Présent de l'Architecture et de l'Urbanisme,* Crès et Cie, Paris, 1930; as a comparison the reader may be interested in his memoirs on the occasion of his first visit to the United States in *When the Cathedrals Were White,* Reynal & Hitchcock, New York, 1947.

11. For the modern history of the azulejo see Joaquim Cardozo, "Rebirth of the Azulejo" in *Architectural Review,* December, 1946; for the use of azulejos in earlier Brazilian architecture see Mario Barata, *Azulejo no Brasil,* Rio de Janeiro, 1955.

12. Professor Mario Barata of the National Faculty of Architecture of Brazil comments on the "messianic" attitude of his students (see *Minutes of the Extraordinary International Congress of Art Critics,* 1959).

13. See Foreword by Lucio Costa in Stamo Papadaki, *The Work of Oscar Niemeyer,* Reinhold, New York, 1950.

14. It is a practice in Brazil to entrust the architect with the establishment of preliminary and working drawings, but the supervision of actual building construction is performed by a responsible engineer. Also, because of certain forms of financing the construction of a building—often through annual outlays—a great lapse of time may occur between the design of a project and the realization of the building. Thus, most, if not all, the projects are "live" ones, that is to say they will be built or finished at some later date—in contrast with the practice elsewhere according to which a project after a certain time enters the architect's dead files. Hence, it is very difficult to give a definite date to the buildings and projects presented here. Dates usually indicate the establishment of the project except where its construction followed immediately, and then the date indicates the erection of the building.

15. For the aerial tree see Chapter 10 in Gaston Bachelard, *L'Air et les Songes,* José Corti, Paris, 1943; for the subterranean tree, Chapter 9 in *La Terre et les Rêveries de Repos* by the same author, published by José Corti, Paris, 1948; for the sacred tree see Mircea Eliade, *The Myth of the Eternal Return,* Pantheon, New York, 1954.

16. The first contemporary building with a permanent and continuous device as a protection against the sun was, to the best knowledge of the author, designed by Georges Ovide Leclerc and the author. This "sunbreak"—the term had not been coined then—consisted of a series of cantilevered, horizontal, permanent concrete slabs projecting about ten feet from the glass wall and supported by the structural columns of the building. The building was a memorial to Christopher Columbus to be erected in the City of San Domingo and the concrete louvers were to shield the chapel. The project was published first in the Spanish magazine *Arquitectura,* No. 6, Madrid, 1929, but the international competition for the design of the monument took place in 1928. The project was published again later in Alberto Sartoris, *Gli Elementi dell'Architettura Funzionale,* Ulrico Hoepli, Milan, 1932, pp. 275, 276. Incidentally, this is the first project in the modern architectural movement to be planned with a tropical climate in consideration and it is, perhaps, interesting to note the transmutation of forms or the source of the idea. The designers were impressed with the concrete louvers projecting from the clock tower of the Pavilion of Tourism by Robert Mallet-Stevens at the International Exposition of Decorative Arts in Paris, 1925. Those louvers, for the downward direction of the sound, were a version in reinforced concrete of the wooden ones to be found in the bell towers of all major churches. A simple play of the mind substituted light for sound and

Figure 8. Robert Mallet-Stevens, Pavilion of Tourism, Paris, 1925 (photomechanical reproduction of a photograph in the author's collection).

this was made easy by the fact that the Pavilion's louvers were horizontal and not directed towards the ground, perhaps for aesthetic reasons.

17. See Sigfried Giedion, *The Work of Affonso Reidy,* Praeger, New York, 1960. The other two architects who collaborated in the design of the Ministry of Education Building were Carlos Leao and Ernani Vasconcellos.

18. See catalog, *Contemporary Sculpture, 2nd Exhibition of the Sculptor's Guild,* Brooklyn Museum, New York, 1938.

19. Alfred Roth, *The New Architecture,* Girsberger, Zurich, 1940.

20. Directly from the surrealist movement we have some drawings (in *Minotaure,* No. 11, 1938, p. 43) by the painter Matta, who started as an architect, and projects by Marcel Jean (in *L'Architecture d'Aujourd'hui,* special issue on art, 1946, p. 27) which are very close to Yves Tanguy landscapes and, of course, we are indebted to the André Breton group for the rediscovery in the late twenties of the work of Gaudí.

21. See "Richtlinien von La Sarraz," reprinted in *Rationelle Bebauungsweisen,* Enlert und Schlosser, Frankfurt, 1931, p. 206.

22. In "Frank Lloyd Wright" with a preface by Henry-Russell Hitchcock, *Cahiers d'Art,* Paris, 1928.

23. See Bernard Champigneulle, "Auguste Perret," *Arts et Métiers Graphiques,* Paris, 1959.

24. In *Gli Elementi dell'Architettura Funzionale,* cited above, pp. 465-467.

25. Other painters with whom Niemeyer often collaborated are Cavalcanti and Saldanha; the latter created a remarkable mural for the auditorium of the school in Belo Horizonte (plate 45) showing a particular understanding in the interpretation of the shape of the wall.

26. *Crusade* is the title of the last book of Le Corbusier in the "Collection de l' Esprit Nouveau," Crès et Cie, Paris, 1932—but his whole professional life is devoted to a crusade.

27. See K. Lönberg-Holm and C. Theodore Larson, *Planning for Productivity,* International Industrial Relations Institute, The Hague, 1940, and *Development Index,* University of Michigan, Ann Arbor, 1953; Frederick Kiesler, "The Genetics of Design," *Architectural Record,* Sept., 1939, pp. 59-75.

28. See Catalog of Exhibition "Antagonismes" at the Pavillon de Marsan, Paris, 1960, under the auspices of Fleischmann-Nabocov, texts by Julien Alvard.

29. See Mircea Eliade, *Traité d'Histoire des Religions,* Payot, Paris, 1959, chapter on sacred space.

30. Joaquim Cardozo, an engineer with an unusual cultural background and understanding, often collaborated with Niemeyer, specifically in the Casino and Yacht Club of Pampulha (plates 129-134), the Boavista Bank (plates 7-11), the Diamantina Hotel (plates 113-119), the Kubitschek Housing Complex (plates 94-97) and the São Paulo Exposition (plates 60-64).

31. For the symbolism of the number three see Dr. Ludwig Paneth, *La Symbolique des Nombres dans l'Inconscient,* Payot, Paris, 1953, and Matyla Ghyka, *Philosophie et Mystique du Nombre,* Payot, Paris, 1952. There was another city which was planned to be the seat of Government, a new capital, showing a triadic symbolism: Constantinople. Saint Sophia, the Imperial Palace and the Hippodrome, representing God, the Emperor and the People, were grouped together, but the triangular form was hardly discernible because of the enormous differences in size and shape of the components. The symbolism in this instance was more suggestive through the interdependent activity than through visual impact.

CHRONOLOGY

1907 Born Oscar Niemeyer Soares Filho, December 15, in Rio de Janeiro

1930 Entered the National School of Fine Arts (now Faculdade Nacional de Arquitectura) in Rio de Janeiro to study architecture. While a student, he worked in the office of the architect Lucio Costa

1934 Received the "Architect's Diploma"

1936 Worked with Le Corbusier for about four weeks in May and June on the Ministry of Education Building and on a preliminary plan for a new campus for the National University
Began independent practice

1937 Built a maternity clinic for the "Obra do Berco," Rio de Janeiro, his first executed work[14]

1939 Visited New York in connection with his design for the Brazilian Pavilion at the New York World's Fair (in collaboration with Lucio Costa and with interior displays by Paul Lester Wiener)
Made honorary citizen of New York City by Mayor Fiorello LaGuardia
Elected chief architect in charge by the design group for the Ministry of Education Building in Rio de Janeiro

1940 Organized the Brazilian Industrial Exhibition in Buenos Aires for the Brazilian Government
Designed the "Grand Hotel" in Ouro Preto, a colonial town in Minas Gerais

1941 Won a competition conducted by the Ministry of Education for the "National Athletic Center" in Rio de Janeiro

1942 Built the Pampulha (Belo Horizonte) group of buildings: Casino, Yacht Club of Minas Gerais, Restaurant "Baile" and the Church of Saint Francis of Assisi
Built his own house (the first) in the Gavea section of Rio de Janeiro

1943   Completion of the Ministry of Education Building

1944   Designed an amusement center at the Rodrigos de Freitas Lagoon (commissioned by the Mayor of Rio de Janeiro)

1946   Designed the headquarters for the "Boavista Bank" in Rio de Janeiro

1947   Won the competition for the "Aeronautical Training Center" at São José dos Campos, State of São Paulo, a vast complex of shops, educational buildings and extensive housing for students, instructors, and technicians
Served in New York as a member of the advisory committee for the United Nations Headquarters

1949   Designed the headquarters for the printing firm "O Cruzeiro" in Rio de Janeiro
Elected honorary member of the American Academy of Arts and Sciences

1950   Designed the manufacturing center for the food processing industry of "Carlos de Britto, S. A." in São Paulo, his first industrial complex
Completed the project for the "Quitandinha" apartment hotel in Petropolis
Completed the "Montreal" building in São Paulo

1951   Designed the "Governor Kubitschek," two housing blocks in Belo Horizonte (built in 1958)
Completed a hotel, school and club in Diamantina
Made the preliminary drawings for the São Paulo Fourth Centennial Exposition (inaugurated in 1954), in collaboration with Helio Uchoa, Zenon Lotufo, Eduardo Kneese de Mello, Gaus Estelita and Carlos Lemos

1952   Designed the hospital "Sul America" in Rio de Janeiro (completed in 1959)

1953   Designed the headquarters for the "Mineiro da Producao" Bank in Belo Horizonte
Built his own house (the second) in the Canoa section of Rio de Janeiro

1954   Designed a secondary school in Belo Horizonte

1955   Designed the headquarters of the Getulio Vargas Foundation for Public Administration Research in Rio de Janeiro
Designed a housing block for the 1957 International Reconstruction Fair in Berlin (Hansa) as one of fifteen architects invited to participate in the program

Visited many European capitals, including Berlin, Warsaw and Moscow during a prolonged trip

Launched the magazine *Modulo* and published the first issue in March, 1955

1956   Appointed technical adviser to Novacap (the Authority for the New Capital of Brazil)

Designed preliminary plans for the presidential palace, the "Brasilia Palace Hotel" and some temporary buildings on the site of Brasilia

1957   Represented Novacap as one of the six judges of the competition for a plan for Brasilia

Appointed chief architect of Novacap, gave up his private architectural practice and moved to the site of Brasilia

1960   After the official inauguration of Brasilia on April 21, returned to Rio de Janeiro to resume his private practice but continued as architectural adviser to Novacap

BIBLIOGRAPHICAL NOTE

For the SOCIAL HISTORY of Brazil see Note 6. LITERARY WORKS with strong ethnic background: Machado de Assis, *Philosopher or Dog?*, Noonday Press, N. Y., 1954; Jorge Amado, *Captains of the Sands, Bahia of All Saints, Violent Earth, The Roads of Hunger*, Martins, São Paulo, all translated into English, French, and German but not published in the United States; *The Diary of Helena Morley*, translated by Elizabeth Bishop, Farrar, Straus and Cudahy, N. Y., 1957. GENERAL: "Perspectives of Brazil," an *Atlantic Monthly* Supplement, 1956, edited by Carleton Sprague Smith and sponsored by *Perspectives USA*, a Ford Foundation undertaking. BOOKS ON BRAZILIAN ARCHITECTURE (where the work of Oscar Niemeyer is generously illustrated): Philip L. Goodwin and Elizabeth Mock, *Brazil Builds*, The Museum of Modern Art, N. Y., 1943; Alberto Sartoris, *Encyclopédie de l'Architecture Moderne, Ordre et Climat Américain*, Ulrico Hoepli, Milan, 1954; Henry-Russell Hitchcock, *Latin American Architecture since 1945*, The Museum of Modern Art, N. Y., 1955; Henrique E. Mindlin, *Modern Architecture in Brazil*, Reinhold, N. Y., 1956. Brazilian architecture (including Niemeyer's work) was the subject of many special issues of ARCHITECTURAL PERIODICALS, namely: *L'Architecture d'Aujourd'hui*, September, 1947; October, 1952; October-November, 1958 (special presentation on Brasilia); *The Architectural Review*, March, 1944; October, 1950; October, 1954; *The Architectural Forum*, November, 1947; *Progressive Architecture*, April, 1947; December, 1956; April, 1957; *Modulo, a Magazine of Brazilian Architecture and Plastic Arts*, published since 1955 in Rio de Janeiro by a group under Oscar Niemeyer, appearing irregularly (about three issues a year) and presenting a selection of current architectural projects in Brazil. OTHER PERIODICALS: *Brasilia*, a monthly publication of the Public Relations Department of Novacap (Companhia Urbanizadora da Nova Capital do Brasil) has appeared since January, 1957, and presents buildings in progress at the new capital; *Habitat, a Magazine of the Arts of Brazil*, published since 1950 by the director of the art museum of São Paulo; *Mirador, Panorama of Industrial Civilization*, Buenos Aires, October, 1958 (presentation on Brasilia). ARTICLES ON OSCAR NIEMEYER: "Oscar Niemeyer" by E. Bergen in *Bouwen en Wonen*, Antwerp, January, 1957, pp. 34-36; "Oscar Niemeyer, Architetto Brasiliano," signed F. M., in *Quaderni della Società Generale Immobiliare di Lavori di Utilità Pubblica ed Agricola*, Rome, September, 1957, pp. 28-54. ARTICLES BY OSCAR NIEMEYER expressing his thoughts on architecture are to be found in practically all issues of *Modulo* (with English, French and German translations); also in *L'Architecture d'Aujourd'hui*, October-November, 1958, the article entitled "Témoignages," p. 55; in *Le Corbusier: Oeuvres Complètes, 1938 & 1946*, Girsberger, Zurich, the article entitled "Ce qui manque à notre Architecture," p. 90. MONOGRAPHS ON NIEMEYER: Stamo Papadaki, *The Work of Oscar Niemeyer*, Reinhold, N. Y., 1950 (also in Japanese translation as a special issue of *Kokusai-Kenchiku*, Tokyo, May, 1952); and *Oscar Niemeyer: Works in Progress*, Reinhold, N. Y., 1956, by the same author.

INDEX

Numbers in regular roman type refer to text pages; *italic* figures refer to the plates.

SOURCES OF ILLUSTRATIONS

Marcel Gautherot, Rio de Janeiro: 27, 30, 32, 33, 34, 41, 83, 84, 85, 86, 88, 89, 90, 96, 97, 98, 99, 100, 102, 104, 105, 106, 107, 108, 118, 119, 120, 121, 123, 124, 125, 126, 132, 135
Foto Jerry, Rio de Janeiro: 127, 143, 145
R. Landau, Rio de Janeiro: 11, 15
F. S. Lincoln, New York: 57, 58
Toper, Belo Horizonte: 141

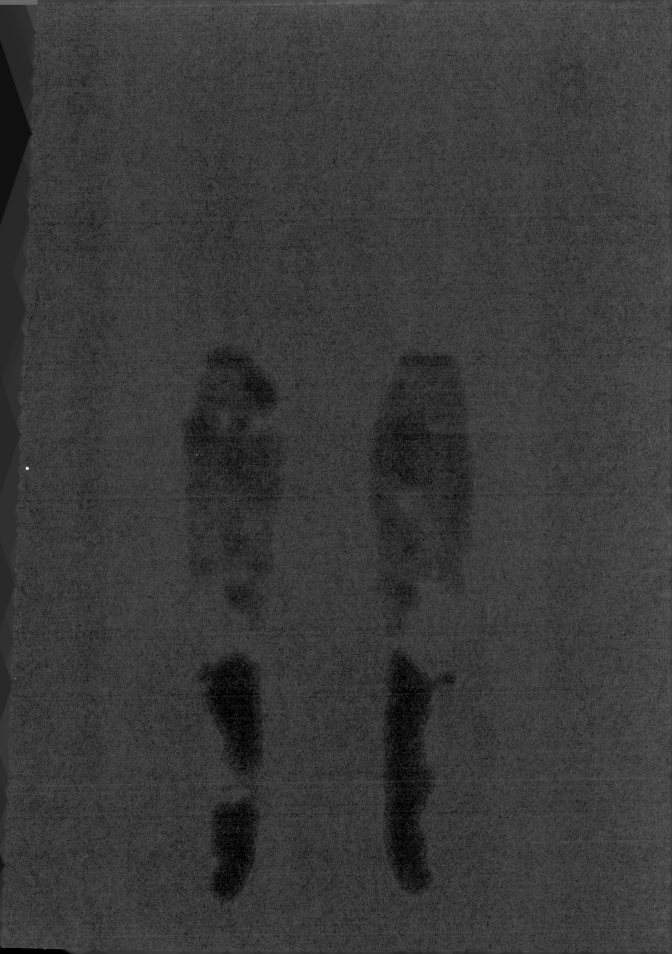